Fragile but Fierce

A Quote Collection

Nikki Rowe

BALBOA.PRESS
A DIVISION OF HAY HOUSE

Balboa Press books may be ordered through booksellers or by contacting:

Balboa Press
A Division of Hay House
1663 Liberty Drive
Bloomington, IN 47403
www.balboapress.com.au
1 (877) 407-4847

Because of the dynamic nature of the Internet, any web addresses or links contained in
this book may have changed since publication and may no longer be valid. The views
expressed in this work are solely those of the author and do not necessarily reflect the
views of the publisher, and the publisher hereby disclaims any responsibility for them.

The author of this book does not dispense medical advice or prescribe the use of any
technique as a form of treatment for physical, emotional, or medical problems without the
advice of a physician, either directly or indirectly. The intent of the author is only to offer
information of a general nature to help you in your quest for emotional and spiritual well-
being. In the event you use any of the information in this book for yourself, which is your
constitutional right, the author and the publisher assume no responsibility for your actions.

Any people depicted in stock imagery provided by Getty Images are models,
and such images are being used for illustrative purposes only.
Certain stock imagery © Getty Images.

Interior Image Credit: NikkiJade Creations

Print information available on the last page.

ISBN: 978-1-5043-2081-8 (sc)
ISBN: 978-1-5043-2082-5 (e)

Balboa Press rev. date: 03/05/2020

Acknowledgements

To my son, Xavier

My spirit is free because of you, lifetime after lifetime we find each other.

Thankyou for walking this earth alongside me, caring for me, fulfilling me with unconditional love. Your resilience in the face of adversity gives me strength, your laughter in moments of chaos give me peace. It's because of you I breathe easier. It's because of you, I promised myself I'd never stray to far from my own soul. Thankyou for being my best friend.

To my Mum, Lyn

The world is a better place because of your existence, my world wouldn't be so enriched without a mum like you. You have taught me to be the woman I am, supported me, encouraged me, uplifted me but more importantly been the most admirable woman to look up to. If I turn out to be half the woman you are, I'll be proud. You give me purpose, reason and people meaning. I will never stop counting my blessings of how lucky we are to have the soul connection we do. You're not only my mum, but my best friend and again we meet for another journey, earthbound.

To my soul sister, Amber

You came into my world, when most of it walked out. You brought my spirit back to life, it's you I thank for giving me hope to shine. Thank-you for saving me every single time. The world is a big place with many different humans, how rare it is to find those who sing your tune, speak your language and dance your dance. I am one of the lucky ones, to embrace a friendship many seek their entire lives for.

She is like a wildflower;
she spent her time allowing herself to grow.
Not many knew of her struggle,
but eventually all knew of her light.

Some days, I am the artist;
other days, I am the art.
When life gets really weird,
I tend to become both.

Wildflower, pick up your pretty little
head. Your life is not over;
your dreams are not dead.

Don't let hollow heroes distract
you from saving yourself.

She is like a butterfly:
pretty to look at but hard to catch.

She was born to be free;
let her run wild in her own way,
and you will never lose her.

No one knows what you have been through
or what your pretty little eyes have seen,
but I can assure you
whatever you have conquered,
it shines through your mind.

Wild women are an unexplainable
spark of life.
They ooze freedom and seek awareness.
They belong to nobody but themselves
yet give a piece of who they are
to everyone they meet.
If you have met one, hold onto her.
She'll allow you into her chaos,
but she'll also show you her magic.

She has fought many wars—most internal,
the ones you battle alone.
For this, she is remarkable.
She is a survivor.

She was like the sun;
she knew her place in the world.
She would shine on again regardless of all
the storms and changeable weather.
She wouldn't adjust her purpose
for things that pass.

Solitude is where I place my chaos to rest
and awaken my inner peace.

I am a wild woman;
it would take a warrior to tame my spirit.

You're growing, and that scares people.
It frightens the shit out of them because they know if they
don't grow within themselves,
you will move forward without them.
When and if this happens,
don't you dare settle to suit the mould.
Have the courage to live without one.

I will not dilute my senses to
match your perception;
take it or leave it.
I'm a girl with magic hands.

A wild spirit like hers never stays too long,
but her essence never really leaves.

Some moments can be painfully
uncanny like that;
some moments last a lifetime,
whilst others have an expiry date.

You stop revisiting memories
when you outgrow the people
you made them with.

Be aware of the selfish givers,
those who do something for a hidden fee.

How wrong we are to ignore our hearts
to follow a familiar path.

Many speak to her,
but she is looking for the one who
knows her soul's language.

There's something about kindred spirits.
You meet them, and for a moment,
no matter how ugly,
the world makes sense.
They bring a sense of clarity and freedom
with just one conversation—
just enough to remind you of who you are.

They'll look for you in a bed of roses,
having never really known you at all.
For you'll never be found in a
perfectly rendered garden.
You're a wildflower in this world.

I am not a girl who will lie in your diamonds, but I will run through the flowers of the seeds we plant together.

Some are born to play it safe;
others are born to live it wild.

The greatest asset you can own
is an open heart.

We all have a soul family,
the ones who ignite and support our truth.
They feed something in us we weren't aware
we needed before we met them.
They make us face ourselves and
become more raw and authentic.
We'll roam but never too far from each other,
for the invisible thread of connectedness—
once opened—can never be locked.
They are the ones who will see us through all
the important days of our lives, no matter
what tributes and trials we face.
They'll just be there in presence, synchronicity, or spirit.

What a rebellious act it is to
love yourself naturally
in a world of fake appearances.

Happiness will be fleeting
if you constantly search for it in places
that can be taken away;
it's an inside job.

You are here—alive and awake—
and for whatever reasons you have
fought your battles,
the time will come when you are
forced to focus on the strengths
that have brought you back up when the
whole world has knocked you down.
That's where the virtue in self grows.

The chaos doesn't end;
you kind of just become the calm.

Your heartbreak has no time frame;
you can't rush healing.

When your heart truly mends,
it doesn't let the same people in twice.

You won't forget a woman like that—
easily, anyway.
Once you cross paths with magic,
it's hard to see life the same.

Some days I like to wander to old
and worn-out places,
forests ripped apart by man and
streams that carry stagnant water,
where once was a flow.
There is a sense of clarity in these places,
a reflection of who I am
or at least who I have been:
broken at the hands of another but finding my beautiful.

Stories are made about girls like you—
the wild ones,
those faces that smile in the midst of chaos.

The creative mind can turn chaos
into a masterpiece
and call it art.

If you are not more alive when in love,
then you, my friend,
are in love with the wrong one.

We all have the power within us
to make something of ourselves;
the thing is
very few people believe it.

Sometimes I feel immortal;
I am caught up in my own little world,
creating piece after piece.
I guess that's the alchemy
of an expressive soul;
we take no moments for granted.
One day we will be gone,
but who we were whilst we lived
will always remain.

Be an individual;
let out the self that hides away at the
expense of others' approval.

Give focus only to what you want to see expand;
anything else is nonsense.

If you live every day with the capacity
to stretch yourself past
the limitation and structure,
you will find boundless opportunities
in all the places
that once scared you.

Fierce and fragile can coexist;
never underestimate the power of the two.

There is a quiet little revolution
in choosing yourself
for the first time.

Don't let someone rearrange your path
because they lost sight of their own.

Many die long before their departure date,
through ignorance of living a life
they never wanted to be a part of
but are too afraid to change.

There is nothing more powerful
than this moment you're living now,
more powerful than your
convictions and truths.
Spend time with what your heart desires
and your soul screams for.
Life ends a day before we know it.
That's why it's so important to chase
everything that matters to us.

Oh, darling, you're only too wild for
those who are too tame;
don't let their opinions change you.

They talk about hell like it's
another world away,
yet all the devils are here and
we're just puppets in their play.

How delicately fragile this journey must be
if only one small moment can alter the
direction of your life forever.

Maybe it has nothing to do with bad
timing and that's why the universe
will never let us align;
no matter how strong the soul pull,
some stories just aren't mine.

People will come, and they will go.
You have to learn to be OK with both.

It's always easier to walk
down nostalgia lane
when you haven't planned a future;
it'll be a cycle on repeat until
you change its focus.

Some friendships will end;
there is no promise on the length of the journey shared,
nor are there any measurements
of depths reached.
But one thing above all is certain:
whether they are here for a
long time or short,
their presence shifted you, and that
alone can sometimes be enough.

I can't guarantee you this life will
spare you of heartache and despair,
but I can remind you
that within you is an unshakeable strength
that will see you through some terrible days.
Utilise those parts within yourself
when the going gets a little too rough.

I said, "But I have to go;
there are many places calling my name."

I am a language lost in translation
between foreign lands;
not many understand my journey.
It's not one for the common man.

The only cure to all this madness
is to dream far and wide.
If opportunity doesn't knock,
build a goddamn door.
If the shoe doesn't fit, don't force it.
If the journey you're travelling
seems far-fetched and out of reach, continue on it.
Great things come to the risk-takers.
Last but not least, live today—
right here in the now.
You'll thank your future self for it later.

Be honest with yourself
about what's real and what hurts;
self-awareness is a powerful tool
to navigate your life.
Grow the connection with your
intuition, frequency, and vibes.

I am a voice for the damaged souls,
the ones who bear the pain of the earth.
So many sad stories with smiling faces
teaching a life metaphor;
your struggles
should never define your worth.

There is only one place I want to go,
and it's all the places I have never been.

If you try to tame her, she will fly away
because pretty little spirits like her
never like to be caged.

You can't expect someone to understand your journey
when they've hardly lived one of their own.

If you live every day with the capacity to
stretch yourself past limitation
and structure,
you will find boundless opportunities
in all the places
that once scared you.

Trust what your instinct is telling you;
it's your soul's voice pointing you in
the right direction.

You'll reach a comfort zone in your life
and start to wonder how you got there.
How did you miss the signposts that redirected your truth?
Don't feel so guilty.
You know when you're meant to know,
and I guess that's the thing
they don't teach you growing up.
Pain is inevitable,
but staying the same is a choice.
Don't question why you are ready
for change. Question why
you stayed the same for so long.

Don't let someone rearrange your path
because they lost sight of their own.

Tomorrow when you wake up,
be aware of how you dress your thought;
if your inner being isn't beautiful,
neither are you.

The world tried to cage her,
but they didn't know those walls
gave her the courage to fly.

You have to keep doing it,
even if no one is watching.
The best artists live from expression,
not chasing impressions.

Let there be room in your heart
for the unimaginable;
serendipity has a way of showing up
just when you feel like giving up.

Master the chaos within yourself,
and I promise
you will gain the strength to
withstand any storm.

I think sometimes,
despite our wise choices
and good intentions,
some things are up to fate and
we learn to play our part the best we can.

Solitude is where I place my chaos
to rest and awaken my inner peace.

The creative mind can turn chaos
into a masterpiece
and call it art.

She wore her battle scars like wings;
looking at her, you would never know
that once upon a time,
she forgot how to fly.

Don't suffocate your spirit for lessons that
were only passing through spring.

I don't wear the opinion of others anymore;
I learnt to dress myself.

We all have the power within us
to make something of ourselves;
the thing is very few people believe it.

Accept where you are,
accept what you have,
do what you can with that, and
let it be enough.

Your attitude will either make or break you;
we can't choose the tragedies
that enter our lives,
but we can choose how we
want them to change us.

I had less and became more.

Open your mind a little;
don't believe everything you see,
read, or hear.
The world is so caught up in trying to
avoid the topics that matter that
you'll lose yourself trying to become anything like it.

Dismantle your wounds
so you stop living by them.

Leave me with less,
and watch me build an entire empire
with your shadow.

Standing alone scares people.
It means they have to be themselves,
and more often than not,
people haven't the slightest clue
who they've been all this time.
That's why people stay the same,
because it's a frightening choice
to step away from the crowd.

Never question yourself
to satisfy those living blindly under
the false masks of life.

Stories are made about girls like you,
those rare ones who smile
in the midst of chaos.

I don't want fleeting
friendships or relationships.
Give me fleeting moments in coffee shops
and walks by the water.
I will never be satisfied with empty kinships
that are fleeting and undecided.
Those connections are
what make us humans,
and I dare not settle my wild little heart
for something of so little depth.

You have to learn where your
weaknesses end and your strengths start,
or you'll spend the rest of your life
focusing on all that falls apart.

Wild ones like us never stay too long,
but our essence never really leaves.

Spend time alone and often;
touch base with your soul.

I don't want ordinary; I will tire easily of that.
My restless spirit needs someone who knows
how to lead my stubborn heart
into adventure.
Give me 9–5 comfort and mediocre,
and I'll leave more quickly than I entered.
I know not much about love,
but I've experienced a lot about what it isn't.

In the end, I was always my own hero;
I never had the chance
to be saved by someone else.

They'll tell you you're mad,
that you see life in a strange way,
whilst they eat their toast, dress for work,
and leave by the same time,
for the same place,
every day.

I think it's fair to say that age will never define wisdom;
only experience can do that.
And sometimes experience alone
isn't enough to make a man get on his knees and pray.

I've been fed to wolves,
my soul experiencing
near death so many times.
Having minimal hardship is far better
than being completely *fucked* by life,
by these words.
These goddam words save me every time.
A little slice of poetic notion,
a sweet little reminder
that in pain there is life.

They'll look for you in a bed of roses,
having never really known you at all.
For you'll never be found
in a perfectly tendered garden.
You are a wildflower of this world.

Isn't it ironic
I learnt the most about balance
when I lost the use of one leg?

Don't underestimate the ability of a woman
who has lived on nothing but survival to
rise. If she can master the hurricane,
what makes you think
rainbows won't be named after her?

I've cheated death a few times;
it's like life doesn't want me to live,
but death isn't ready to unite.

She is not what you're used to,
and maybe that scares you a little;
you always admire a strong one
until her truth brings you to your knees.

I am both the wild and the flower;
if you come really close,
you'll learn about both.

Our souls speak a language
that is beyond human understanding—
a connection so rare
the universe won't let us part.

Printed in the United States
By Bookmasters